7
Steps to Riches

Erick Walk

Table of Contents

Introduction

Step 1: Assessing Your Financial Situation   1

Step 2: Picking Your Assets   23

Step 3: Collecting Information   62

Step 4: Taking Action. Starting Investing   71

Step 5: Expanding Your Investments   80

Step 6: Diversifying Your Portfolio   84

Step 7: Aiming for Durable Passive Income Generating Assets   89

Conclusion   98

© Copyright 2014 by Erick Walk – Rado Publishers - All rights reserved.

This document is geared towards providing exact and reliable information in regards to the topic and issue covered. The publication is sold with the idea that the publisher is not required to render accounting, officially permitted, or otherwise, qualified services. If advice is necessary, legal or professional, a practiced individual in the profession should be ordered.

- From a Declaration of Principles which was accepted and approved equally by a Committee of the American Bar Association and a Committee of Publishers and Associations.

In no way is it legal to reproduce, duplicate, or transmit any part of this document in either electronic means or in printed format. Recording of this publication is strictly prohibited and any storage of this document is not allowed unless with written permission from the publisher. All rights reserved.

The information provided herein is stated to be truthful and consistent, in that any liability, in terms of inattention or otherwise, by any usage or abuse of any policies, processes, or directions contained within is the solitary and utter responsibility of the recipient reader. Under no circumstances will any legal responsibility or blame be held against the publisher for any reparation, damages, or monetary loss due to the information herein, either directly or indirectly.

Respective authors own all copyrights not held by the publisher.

The information herein is offered for informational purposes solely, and is universal as so. The presentation of the information is without contract or any type of guarantee assurance.

The trademarks that are used are without any consent, and the publication of the trademark is without permission or backing by the trademark owner. All trademarks and brands within this book are for clarifying purposes only and are the owned by the owners themselves, not affiliated with this document.

Legal Disclaimer – While this book provides effective steps for building up wealth it does not guarantee in any way any forms of financial gains as these would be dependable on numerous external factors.

Introduction

We all want financial security. We work hard so that we can provide for our needs and the needs of our family. We save money to prepare for the unexpected expenses in the future. We also want to make our money work for us to gain passive income and to take our piece of the pie from the growth of the economy. Most of us though, do not know how to start doing this.

The process of becoming rich remains a mystery to a lot of people. They work hard all their lives and yet, they do not get to enjoy the fruits of their labor. The book *"7 Steps to Riches"* aims to change that. This book will help you uncover the mystery to accumulating wealth. It contains proven steps and strategies on how to become rich in 7 easy steps.

In this book, we will discuss 7 simple steps you can follow to become rich. You will be given useful tips on investing in different types of assets to reach your financial goals. It gives you insights on how you can manage your money so that you will always have something left to invest.

We will also discuss how you can start investing, and the different passive income generating assets you can put your money in. While the tips provided here may not make you rich overnight, you will notice how your wealth will grow over time.

Let's get started!

Step 1

Assessing Your Financial Situation

The best way for you to start is by examining your current financial situation. You will need to know where you are now financially, so that you will have an idea on the best options available for you. In this step, you will learn to map out all your financial assets. You will also learn the roles of each of these assets to your journey in achieving your financial freedom.

Setting Your Financial Goal

Many people are in love with the idea of becoming rich. In their minds, they picture a luxurious lifestyle, vacationing in exotic places, eating in expensive restaurants, and buying luxury items. This image however, is not what being rich is all about. The richest people in the world do not necessarily own multiple luxury cars or homes in the hills of Los Angles and the penthouses of New York.

The richest people in the world do not even think of buying luxury items. Instead, they are focused on being productive. They are focused on making more money, day-in and day-out. This idea may seem ridiculous to most people. The average person would want to retire once he becomes rich, and most people do not understand why the rich still keep working for money.

To understand why they are doing this, you should think of the rich as an extremely goal oriented bunch. They had set their financial goals in the past and they are doing everything in their power to reach them. This is why they wake up every morning just like regular Joes and Janes, suit up, and go to work.

You should also have the same mindset even if you are not yet as rich as you wish to be. You should set your financial goals and work as hard as you can to reach them. This is the first and most important principle of becoming rich. You must maximize your earning potential by being wise on how you use your time.

To set your financial goals, start by thinking why you want to become rich and what your definition of being rich is. Many poor souls do not think about their reasons for working or for investing. This approach is a motivational pitfall.

While it is impossible to put one hundred percent of your time on your financial goals, you can improve your performance by gathering data on how you spend your time and adjust your behavior to optimize for success. You should do all these to increase your chances of achieving your goals.

Before you move on to the next section, think of the reason why you want to become rich. Ideally, you should write this down. When doing this, consider your dreams when you were still young and your dreams for each of your loved ones.

Understanding Your Cash Flow

The cash flow is the most basic of all financial processes. Cash flow is the movement of money that is within your control. Many startup businesses fail because they do not know how to manage their cash flow.

In the same way, many people struggle financially because of a lack of understanding of how money moves in and out of their possession. In this section, we will have a short discussion on how you can become more aware of your personal and household cash flow, as well as how you can optimize it to increase your savings and investment funds.

Income and Expenses

To start learning about your cash flow, you will first need to record two important figures, your monthly income and expenses. By simply recording these two monthly figures, you will already know if you can become rich. Rich people have a significantly higher income compared to their expenses. Because of this, they can save a big chunk of their income. Let us first discuss the negative part of your personal cash flow, your expenses.

- *Expenses* - Expenses cause money to go out of your pocket and your overall control. It transfers ownership. Thus, the money you pay for expenses can no longer be considered yours.

  Some types of expenses are important, such as the money we use to cover for our rent, food, utilities, transportation and our other needs. Expenses become less important when they are spent on unnecessary items.

  In your cash flow sheet, expenses should always come with a negative sign. It is subtracted from your monthly income so that you become more aware of the impact of your spending in your long term financial goals.

  It goes without saying that we want to keep our expenses low. The lesser our expenses are, the greater our potential savings will be.

  As much as possible, we also want to keep expenses lower than our income. If you fail to do this, you end up with a deficit for the recorded period. A person who always spends more than he earns will end up broke.

- *Income* - Income is the opposite of expenses. It is the total amount of money that you earned for a certain period. In this case, we record the monthly income. For most people, the income comes from their salary. This type of income, though is fixed. You cannot rely solely on it to make you rich. You will need to turn your excess income into financial assets that will grow in value over time, and will create passive income for you.

In your monthly cash flow chart, the income should include all the money that you received in a given month. This includes your salary as well as other one-time earnings. If you did some extra projects on the side, for example, and you received payment for them, you should include this income in your chart as well. In some months when you earn more money, your income will be bigger.

If some unfortunate circumstance happens like if you lose your job, your monthly income will also decrease. To become rich, you will need to maximize the time that you spend on productive activities and you need to make use of the financial opportunities available to you to earn passive income.

Calculating Your Monthly Net income or Deficit

As mentioned earlier, you should subtract your monthly expenses from your monthly income. If the resulting figure is positive, you will end up with some savings for the month. If it is negative, on the other hand, you will need to make adjustments in the following month to prevent it from happening again.

Deficits will eat away from your saved funds. If you end up in a deficit every month, this means that your financial resources are slowly getting depleted. You do not want this to happen. To prevent it, you need to keep your expenses to a minimum. Here are some of the things you can do:

- Make a list of the things you regularly spend on - Becoming aware of your financial habits is always the first step to becoming rich. Most of the time, it is your lack of awareness that makes you spend too much. By listing your daily expenses, you will learn which types of spending are eating away the most of your income.

- Identify the expenses you can live without - Each one of us has different values. A parent for example, values things and experiences that will make his or her children happy. You will need to decide which of the items you spend on regularly you value the most and which ones you can live without.

- Create a holistic budget - The secret to proper budgeting is moderation. You will feel bored and unmotivated if you only spend on your basic needs. An extremely frugal lifestyle may also affect your relationships with the people around you. Your kids may feel unmotivated to go to school. Your friends may look down on you.

  To prevent this from happening, you should plan your budget so that it covers all the things plus a regular dose of entertainment and enjoyment.

- Let all the important people in your life know about your financial goals - You may feel embarrassed at first, but coming clean with your goal of becoming rich is the best way for you to retain your relationships with your friends and family. You should choose a few people you trust with this information, and tell them that you are saving up for something or that you are planning to invest.

  Try it first with your own family members. Some of them may not understand immediately why you are being frugal and why you are saving most of your money. If your wife begins to understand that you are doing this for the future of the family however, she may be able to understand whatever financial decisions you make.

After this, communicate your goal with your kids in a way that they will understand. For instance, you can reward them for saving their money. Instead of doing expensive bonding activities, you could explain that spending time somewhere local will be a lot more fun.

Become Aware of All Your Debts

Debt can debilitate you in your quest to achieve financial security. Debt usually comes with interest rates. If you ignore your financial commitments, the interest will pile up. In the worst cases, the monthly payment required by the lender may become difficult to manage.

We do not want this to happen. If you still have a lot of debt, all the gains from your investing efforts may only go to debt payments. Ideally, you should use the majority of your savings to your debt payment first. You should aim to wipe out your debt first before you start investing. In this section, we will discuss the steps on how you can get rid of all of your debts:

1. Put all your debts on paper - Awareness is always the first step to financial intelligence. If you are not aware of the movements of your money, you will never become rich. To get rid of all your debts, you should list them all down in a ledger. Better yet, you could create a spreadsheet file for them.

   Together with the name and a short description of the debt, you should include the principal amount of the debt, its interest rate, and its current size.

2. List your debts from the one with the biggest interest rate to the smallest - The debts with the biggest interest rates grow the fastest. You want to get rid of them first. You need to be aware which ones of your debts are more likely to balloon in size. By listing your debt this way, you will be ready for the next strategy.

3. Learn how much you need to pay - After making a list of your debts, you will need to get the total amount that you need to pay. You will be able to pay them off given enough time. However, you will need to be smart with your approach. You can use free debt payment calculators online to know how much you will need to pay.

   These calculators will ask you for the total amount of you debt, the interest rate, and the deadline you set for paying the debt off.

The calculator will then give you the amount that you should pay monthly so that you will achieve your goal in the timeframe you indicated. If you will not be able to pay the amount given by the calculator, you have the option to increase the duration of payment or to seek financial assistance in paying of your debt.

4. Pay off the debt with the bigger interest rate first - The best strategy for getting rid of your debts is to pay off the one with the biggest interest rate first. You will need to pay the minimum amount allowed in your other debts. After paying them off, you can shift the rest of your debt-payment fund to the one with the biggest interest rate.

5. Seek financial assistance if needed - Some people lose control of their debts, and they can no longer pay them off. If this happens to you, the best option is to seek professional help. Some banks, for example, offer debt consolidation services.

In this type of service, the bank will pay off all of your other debts so that you only owe one institution. They will also set a fixed interest rate on the consolidated debt. The interest rate is usually lower than the average interest rate of your original debts.

While this may seem like the best option, you will need to study it carefully before you pull the trigger. Debt consolidation services are recorded in your credit history. If creditors in the future see that you have consolidated your debt in the past, this may affect the interest rates of your future loans.

Now that debts are out of the way, let's discuss how you can actually build wealth. Let's start by becoming aware of all of your assets:

Listing Your Financial Assets

The first step in learning about your financial situation is to make a list of all your financial assets. These include all the things and properties you own as well as your cash assets. Here are some of the things that you can add to your list:

Non-Liquid Assets

Let's first discuss the types of non-liquid types of assets. Non-liquid assets refer to things and funds that do have monetary value but cannot be turned into cash instantly. Unlike your money in the bank, you cannot just cash out these types of assets.

Instead, you will need to find buyers and sell them, or wait for the investment to mature before you can turn them into cash. These assets are not easy to sell. Here are some of the examples of non-liquid assets that you may already own:

1. *Real Properties* - Some types of properties tend to maintain their financial value after you buy them. The most common are real properties. If you own pieces of land, houses or buildings, it is possible to earn money from them. The most common way to earn from real estate is by buying and selling. You can sell your real property for a profit.

    Most people though, cannot afford to sell the real property they own. One example of this is your home. You cannot really sell your home or else, you and your family will have nowhere to live. In this case, your property cannot be monetized.

    By learning about real estate, you do have the option to become a real estate investor. This type of investor specializes in the buying, selling and monetization of real properties. You will need to be located in an active city or suburban area to become one though. We will discuss more on this way of investing on future chapters.

2. *Valuable Possessions* - Some things you own may also have financial value. If you own more than one car for example, you can sell one or two of them to increase your liquid assets. Collectors also have items that can be sold to the right buyers. The value of

these types of items, though varies depending on the demand for them.

A lot of people collected baseball cards as kids. Some of them took care of their cards and protected them well from wear and tear. When these collectors grew up, they realized that there is a market for the cards. They were able to sell these items for a profit and turned them into cash.

If you are a collector, you may be sitting on a gold mine. All you have to do is to learn if there is a market for your collection. You will need to find likeminded people who also value the things you collect.

3. *Tied Up Cash* - Some types of financial assets cannot be turned into cash instantly. The best example of this type of assets is your retirement fund. You have money in your fund account, but you will need to wait until you are in your retirement age to access them.

Some people also buy insurance policies that are tied up to investment funds. These types of financial assets earn money over time. However, it is wiser to keep them in the fund while you are still in need of the insurance policy.

Loaned amounts may also fall under this category if it is a long-term loan. The money borrowed is capable of growing, but you will need to wait until the term of the loan is over before you can collect both the capital and the interest.

Most types of investment funds also fall under this category. Many mutual funds, for example, require you to keep the money in the fund for a certain period before you can take the money out. The same goes for debt-based investment instruments like investing in bonds or money markets.

Liquid Assets

Liquid assets refer to the cash and invested funds that are as good as cash. You can take these types of assets and turn them into cash instantly. Your money saved in your savings account is an example. You can take them out today and buy things with them. You do not have to find buyers or to wait for a long period of time to make use of them as currency.

Now let's discuss some of the most common types of liquid assets:

1. *Cash* - Liquid assets are synonymous to cash. You can use them to buy things, properties and even other types of assets. The whole point of this book is to create systems that will make your cash work for you.

   While cash is the most liquid of all types of assets, it is also the type that is most easily wasted. Most people never become wealthy because of poor choices on where to put their money. Instead of saving money or spending it wisely, most people opt to spend their money on consumer products, services and experiences.

Aside from this, the spending power of cash also tends to be affected by many factors that are out of our control. One factor is inflation. The US, for example, has a long term average inflation rate of 3.2%. This simply means that on average, the prices of things and services all over the country increases annually by that rate.

We barely feel the change in prices, but it happens all around us. This change however, does not really have a big effect on the money that we earn and spend on a daily basis. Instead, it has a bigger impact on the cash we store in the bank. Every year, the purchasing power of the money you save in your regular savings account gets weaker. To offset the effects of inflation on your saved cash, you need to put some of them in an investment vehicle that can beat inflation.

2. *Funds in Active Markets* - Not all investments fall in the non-liquid types of assets. Some of them can be instantly turned into cash, though this is only possible for investments that have an active market behind them. The most obvious type

of investment that fall under this category is investing in publicly traded stocks. If your money is tied up in the stock market, you can easily tell your broker to sell your stocks when you need the money. In active stock exchanges, this could happen instantly. You will have your money the next time the market opens.

Becoming aware of all of your assets will help you keep track of your progress. Your goal is to increase the number and the total value of all your assets every year. You can do this by saving part of your income, putting your savings in the right investment vehicles, diversifying your investments, and making the right decisions on when to buy and when to sell.

Roadblocks to Becoming Financially-Independent

If reaching financial security is easy, then why are most people struggling with their finances? The answer is because most people have bad habits and mindsets that prevent them from building their financial empire.

Becoming rich is like building a sturdy home. The foundations need to be strong. The fundamentals of personal finance should be set first. The simple habit of keeping your expenses lower that your income should be made into a personal principle.

Most people, however, do not consider these things important. Their lack of understanding of these fundamental principles leads to bad financial habits that end up eating away on their income. Here are some of the bad habits and mindsets that people have that sabotage their own financial success:

1. *Thinking That You Know Everything That Needs to Be Learned about Money* - We've all been handling money since we were young. From the moment we were given our first lunch or snack money for school, we have been making decisions on how to spend. Most people think that because they have been spending all their lives, they are already wise in handling money. This is the reason why it is almost impossible to teach others the best ways to spend their money.

    If you tell random people simple principles of personal finance, expect to meet violent reactions. Some people will say: "Don't tell me what to do!" or "Mind your own business."

    If you want to become rich, you should not have this kind of mindset. Instead, you should be open to new opportunities of learning. Listen to the advice of people who are knowledgeable about money. After digesting their advice, that's the time when you should decide on whether to dismiss or accept them.

2. *Disregarding the Basic Principles of Personal Finance* - Managing money is no rocket science. We can all learn how to do it properly. Some people who learn how to manage money though, do not practice what they learn. Many people buy and read personal finance books. However, very few of them actually sit down and look for ways on how they can apply the teachings in the book to their own lives.

   You will need to avoid this practice if you want to become rich. You need to practice what you know every day. Keep track of, and minimize, your spending. Maximize your income generating activities. Put your money in the right investment vehicle. These are the basic steps that you need to achieve. Your challenge is how you are going to implement it in your own financial situation.

3. *Falling for Get-Rich-Quick Promises* - As you become richer, it becomes harder to choose the right investment tools to use. We all want the highest yielding investment vehicle. However, most of these vehicles that promise high returns tend to fall short of their commitments.

The worst types of these so called investment vehicles may even turn out to be scams. You should follow the age-old adage in investing: "If its sounds too good to be true, it probably is."

To know if an investment opportunity is too good to be true, check the promised rate of return. The stock market, for example, is considered a generally high-risk market. This means that the potential for earning is high, but the risk of losing is also high. These two factors in investing are always directly proportional. Even though the stock market is considered a high-risk form of investment, on average, investors can only expect around 8% rate of return. It is possible to get a higher percentage of growth in great investing years. However, the average is pulled down by the few years that the market generally ends up losing money. It all balances out in the end.

Scams, on the other hand, promise that they are immune to the principles that govern the rate of return and the risk of the investment. The people behind these scams will promise you that their investment offer will yield returns even higher than the stock market. They will also tell you that the returns are guaranteed.

Do not fall for these tricks. The sooner you know about them, the better. Just remember that all investments come with inherent risks. Your understanding of these risks will help you avoid them.

How Much Can You Invest?

Now that you know your current financial situation, the next step is to find the sweet spot on the amount that you are willing to invest regularly. Investing always involves a certain level of risk. Thus, it is ideal for you to separate your investing money from the rest of your funds.

By this, it means that you should not mix your investment fund with other types of funds you maintain for different purposes. For instance, you should not use the amount that you have set aside for your kid's college fund to invest in the stock market. This goes for all other essential funds like retirement, emergency, and other goal funds.

Ideally, when you decide to invest in the stock market, you should do so using a specific fund. The money should be used solely for this purpose.

Deciding on the Type of Fund to Use

There are two general ways for investing based on the source of the funds that will be used - lump sum and regular investing.

Investing a lump sum amount works best for people who have a large sum of money saved up. Some people, for example, unexpectedly receive a large amount of money. It is common for people to receive a large bonus from work, a sales commission bigger than the usual amount or an unexpected inheritance. When this happens, it is possible to put the majority of the lump sum amount in an investment vehicle to allow you to reach your financial goals faster.

Lump sum investing gives you the opportunity to invest in bigger types of investments with higher returns. Buying real estate as an investment tool, for example, requires you to put up a sizable down payment. You can use the lump sum amount for this.

If the amount is enough, you may also gain access to specialized types of funds. Some hedge funds require a big initial investment before you can join. The lump sum amount you received could also be used as your initial investment in these types of funds.

Regular investing, on the other hand, comes in many forms. The most popular among these is called dollar cost averaging or simply cost averaging. In this method of investing, you can use your regular income like your salary as your source of funds. The majority of investors right now are using this strategy.

Because your investment amount is smaller in this method, you will have limited options for investing. If you are planning to enter the real estate market, for example, you may need to obtain a loan to put up the required amount. You can then use your regular income to pay off the loaned amount.

Your choice of which fund to use varies, according to the types of funds available to you. These two general methods of investing show that there is a viable way for everyone to invest, regardless of whether they have stashed cash or not.

Step 2

Picking Your Assets

Now that you know how much money you have and the source of fund that you will use, it is time to start looking into the types of assets that you can invest in. You can start by exploring the different types of assets available:

Looking for the Available Assets

The types of assets available for you will depend on many factors. Here are some of them:

- *Location* - The country where you wish to invest will significantly affect the number of your investment options. Investing in a mature economy like the US gives you access to the latest types of investment vehicles available. For instance, you will have access to multiple stock exchanges.

    These stock exchanges are divided into smaller niches called indices. The number of indices in a huge economy like the US is significantly bigger compared to smaller countries like the UK.

In contrast, you will not have the same options if you choose to invest in a smaller country. While many smaller countries have mature stock exchanges, the number of companies in these exchanges is fewer. Some industries present in the US markets may not be present.

The US, for example, is known for its booming tech industry. The same industry may not be present yet in smaller exchanges. Some countries that do have this industry may have a significantly fewer companies in them, and their sizes may not be close to that of the companies in the US.

- *Interest* - Your personal interest and experience in different industries will also affect your decision-making process. If you are interested in technology, for instance, you may have an easier time reading financial reports of companies in the tech industry. A person with no experience with technology may not understand the business activities of these types of companies.

  Likewise, your working experience will give you an edge in certain industries. A doctor with expert knowledge about drug companies, for example, should be familiar with the latest news regarding the industry. They may hear of the latest trend in the industry before the regular investor does.

This gives them a chance to act first when there is actionable information. This allows the investor to act before the rest of the market acts, and goes on a buying frenzy.

- *Sum of Money Available for Investing* - The types of assets that you can invest in will also vary, depending on the amount available to you for investing. As stated in the previous chapter, an investor with a lump sum amount has more investing opportunities than those who are using cost averaging. If you have more money available for investing, you will be able to access the premium services in the investing world.

If you are planning to invest in securities, for instance, more money will give you a chance to invest in exclusive funds. In the real estate world, a bigger investment will attract more experienced and well-connected real estate brokers. By attracting these brokers, you will increase the chances of selling your properties.

Checking the Fine Print

In each of the different types of assets that are available to you, there will always be a middleman. Some of these middlemen come in the form of investment companies, while others are individuals who help facilitate the success of your investments.

These middlemen, though are always looking to make a profit from your investment. Many finance professionals work on a commission basis. They are paid from a percentage of the transaction amount. For real estate brokers, for example, they get a percentage of the price of the property they sell. Stock exchange brokers, on the other hand, are paid a commission based on the amount you invest or withdraw from the market.

As an investor, you should do your due diligence to check the fine print regarding the commission rates of the professionals you work with. For big investment companies, the commission rates are usually fixed and non-negotiable. Individual professionals may have a different policy depending on the conditions of the contract that come with the service.

As an investor, you want to keep these rates low, while keeping a fair price based on industry standards. It is important that you only work with professionals who are not overcharging you. They should be transparent when talking about their commission rates and how they make money.

Keep track of the promises made by these professionals, and record them if possible. Your relationships with these people should be put into writing with a contract signed by both parties.

Cutting the Middleman

Eventually, you want to limit the number of people you are working with. If you find a market that you are comfortable with, you can also choose to hire a full time professional to work for you. The amount that you pay freelancers also grows as the size of your investment grows. If your investment is big enough, hiring a professional full time may save you money.

If a person is working for you, you also have the right to demand that he or she only focuses on your investment goals. Many freelance finance professionals work with multiple clients at a time. During busy times of the year, investors with smaller funds may be neglected. The focus of the investment manager will gravitate towards the clients with bigger fund sizes. If you are only a small investor, you may end up not being satisfied with the service.

Common Types of Assets:

Investing in the stock market

The stock market is the most widely discussed type of investment vehicle. Books and movies view the stock market with magical realism. They see it as a place where people can get rich instantly or lose all their fortune in a few minutes. While the events in books and movies are mostly fiction, many of the concepts they use in these stories come from real life experiences. In this book, we will talk about the stock market as just one of the big investment markets. Let's begin by talking about what it is and how it works.

To understand what the stock market is, it is important to first learn what a general market is. In this book we will be talking about many types of markets. Knowing its basic definition will help you understand not just the stock market but also the other ones that will be discussed in the future.

A market is defined as a platform where buyers and sellers of certain products and services meet. In a market, the buyers should be able to see the products being sold and their corresponding prices.

In the stock market, the products bought and sold are the shares of listed companies. Shares refer to representations of ownership of a company. The number of shares that you own is equivalent to a percentage of the value of the company based on the number of shares of that company on the market, and the price of the shares.

Let's say you own 20 shares of a company that has a total of 1,000 shares. This means you own 2% of the said company. As the 2% owner of the company, you have certain privileges. On paper, you should get the equivalent amount of 2% if the company decides to liquidate all of its assets. In some cases, you are also entitled to a percentage of the company's earnings in the period that you own the company shares.

How Do You Make Money?

When investing in the stock market, there are two general ways on how you can earn money - through capital appreciation and dividends.

- *Capital Appreciation* - The first method of earning through stocks is called capital appreciation. The idea is to buy low and sell high. You will find that this method of earning is common among many types of investment vehicles.

    You want to buy shares when the price is low and to sell when the price of the company shares goes up. The bigger the difference is between the original buying price and the selling price, the bigger your profit will be. The number of shares you buy also affects your total earnings. Let's say that the original price of the shares you bought was $100. You bought 1,000 shares while your officemate bought 2,000 shares of the same company.

After a week, the share prices hiked to $105 because of positive news about the company in the press. You and your coworker discussed to pull out your funds and make profit. After selling your shares, you earned a total of $5,000 from your investment ($5 profit * 1,000 shares). Your coworker, on the other hand, earned double that amount at $10,000. Because he bought twice the amount of your shares, his profit is also twice as much.

It is important to note that because your coworker invested double the amount you invested, he risked twice as much money than you. If the market slumped by 1% in the date range, you would have lost $1,000 plus fees. Your officemate, on the other hand, would have lost double that amount of money.

- *Dividends* – Sometimes, company stocks yield dividends. This is one way that the company rewards their loyal investors. The amount of money you usually receive through dividends depends on the number of shares that you have.

  For example, you own 1,000 shares of Company X. The company announced that they will be giving out $0.50 for every share to all common shareholders. This makes you eligible to claim $500 from the dividends that will be released. This type of dividend is usually labelled "dividends per share" or DPS.

At times, there is no fixed dollar amount given. Instead the company bases the DPS on a percentage of the market price of the company stock. In this case, the dividend is usually called dividend yield.

The dividends can also be in the form of additional shares. When a company gives out stock dividends, this may mean that the company may be low on liquid assets. This usually happens when a company known for giving out dividends chooses to reinvest earnings instead of giving out cash dividends.

Generally, a company can only give out dividends when it has made a profit in its previous business dealings. The money given out as dividends usually comes from the excess amount earned by the company.

At the start of every fiscal year, a company usually plots out its projected growth rate. This allows them to set a target revenue to generate, and other metrics for measuring the expansion of the business. At times, a company exceeds the numbers they set, bringing in more cash than they initially anticipated.

The companies that give out dividends choose to use the excess of the money to reward the loyalty of stockholders.

Companies that do not give out dividends may also experience a growth rate and earn more than the usual. However they choose not to distribute the extra earnings back to the investors.

Instead, most of them choose to reinvest the money into the company. If the added capital is used wisely, the reinvestment strategy should lead to better earnings in the following year. If a company's growth is visible to the public, this should reflect in the share's market price.

However, there are times when reinvestment does not necessarily lead to capital appreciation. Because share prices are dictated by the supply and demand of the stock market, many factors come into play in determining the price.

For instance, the current perception of the public regarding investing in stocks can affect the prices. When people are cautious about investing in stocks, there may not be a lot of demand on the market (people wanting to buy stocks). This will lead to lower stock prices.

Even if a company wisely uses its excess cash, its stock price will not increase if the majority of the investing public is not looking to buy stocks. The reinvestment strategy, in this case, will not have a positive effect on the share prices in the short term. While long term investing usually yields better returns, some investors prefer to invest in a company that regularly gives out dividends for short term returns.

These companies are ideal for those who want to make the most of their income now rather than 5 or 10 years from now. For instance, people who are about to retire or already in the retirement age may want to receive cash regularly. They are more likely to invest in companies that regularly hand out dividends.

Types of Stocks

Company stocks come in two types, common stocks and preferred stocks. The price of these two types of stocks differs even within the same company. The rights that come with these two types of shares also vary.

Common Stocks vs. Preferred Stocks

Common stocks are the type of stocks that is commonly available to the investing public. When you tell your broker that you want to invest in the shares of a company, the broker will automatically assume that you are referring to the common shares of that company.

Preferred stocks, on the other hand, are usually issued in limited numbers, making them more exclusive. Preferred stocks usually do not have voting rights. Voting rights refer to the right of the investor to have a say on important company decisions like selecting the company board of directors.

The board usually acts to check and balance the actions of the company leaders like the CEO. The board has the power to replace the CEO if his or her actions do not work for the interest of the investors.

While they may not have the right to vote, preferred stockholders have other special rights. Preferred stocks should be viewed as a more conservative version of a company's common shares. One of its features is that preferred stockholders are given priority when the company decides to distribute cash dividends. Preferred stockholders should receive their piece of the pie first before the common stockholders get theirs.

It is also common for companies to give out dividends solely to preferred stockholders. They do this when the cash given out is not enough to cover both preferred and common shareholders. While common stockholders cannot expect a regular dividend payout, it is common for a company to give regular and scheduled dividend payouts to preferred shareholders.

This rule also applies when the company decides to close shop. In bad times, the company may select the option to end the business and cease operations. In the process, it will need to liquidate all its assets by selling them. When all the assets are liquidated, the company will then distribute the cash proceeds to its investors and creditors.

In the order of receiving money, preferred stockholders are given priority over both common shareholders and creditors.

The movement of prices also varies between common and preferred shares. The market price of both types of shares is subject to the supply and demand of the market. Because common shares are more actively traded though, the fluctuation of the price with this type of share is usually greater.

This can be good or bad, depending on the trend of the price. The price may go up fast when the public perception of the market is good. It may go down when the investors are in a selling frenzy. Because of this fluctuation, common stocks are the preferred type for day traders.

Day traders are players in the stock market that buy and sell stocks in extremely short periods. They are called day traders because the great majority of the stocks that pass through their portfolio are bought and sold within the same day. The presence of these types of players in the market further contributes to the fluctuation in the prices of common shares.

The limited supply of preferred shares also contributes to the fluctuation of its market price. Because this type of share changes ownership less often than common shares, you can count on its price to stay within a certain range. The lack of fluctuation also makes this type of share less attractive to day traders.

Investing in the Stock Market

Most people want to start investing in the stock market but they do not know how to start. The learning curve required at this stage usually causes investors to lose money. To lessen the effect of the learning curve, you should gain access to learning materials about investing in stocks. While this book contains most of the basic information you need to learn, it would help if you find other sources of investing advice.

Aside from this, you will need to find a good broker to work with. Brokers usually work with investment firms and they are paid a commission or a fixed salary for their service. Firms are usually paid per transaction. Some of them would only collect fees for selling stocks. Others will collect them for both buying and selling.

When you start working with an investment firm, they will usually assign a broker for you to manage your account. The performance of the brokers varies, depending on the recruitment process of the firm you are working with and the number of accounts that he handles at once.

Ideally, you want to work with brokers who have fewer accounts on their plate. This will give them more time to talk with you when you need guidance.

You also have the option to work with online investing services. These websites provide a do-it-yourself approach to investing. You can buy and sell stocks without interacting with a single person from the firm. You can make each buying and selling decision yourself based on your research on the companies.

Aside from the independence, using online investing firms also allows you to invest anywhere. You do not need to be in New York to start investing in Wall Street. Instead, you can do all your investing tasks at home or even when you are travelling.

Lastly, online investing accounts usually come with lower service fees compared to their brick-and-mortar counterparts. If you already know what you are doing, you should use these types of accounts rather than pay excessively for a managed investment account.

Investing in Bonds

Aside from investing in stocks, you also have the option to invest in bonds. To understand how bonds work, let's first compare them with stocks.

As mentioned in the previous section, company stocks represent one's stake or ownership in the company. The money you use to buy them buys you a piece of the company.

The money you provided is then used by the company to fund their business activities and growth.

Just like stocks, bonds are also used by a company as a way to raise funds. The funds collected are also used for various business activities. If everything goes as planned, the said business activities lead to growth for the business and to more revenue for the company.

Unlike investing in stocks, buying company bonds does not give you ownership of the company.

You are not entitled to the company's earning and you cannot keep the bonds indefinitely. With stocks, you can hold the stocks longer to increase the potential returns that you can get from it.

While stocks are an equity (ownership) type of investment tool, bonds are usually referred to as debt instruments. They are called debt instruments because the company that issues them is basically borrowing money from you if you choose to buy their bond.

The bond is a piece of paper that acts as a contract between you, the bondholder, and the company that issues it. It acts like a contract because it contains the details of the agreement between you and the company.

It states the amount you gave to the company. From your point of view, this is the capital for your investment. It also states the interest rate that the bond issuer will pay you when the bond matures. The interest rate serves are the company's payment to the bondholder for buying the bonds. It is necessary to motivate investors to buy a company's bond.

Lastly, it states the date on which the bond would be due for redemption. This is called the maturity date. On the maturity date, the issuer of the bond will need to pay the capital amount (the amount borrowed by the company) as well as the interest indicated in the contract.

If the capital amount, for example, is $100 and the interest rate is 5%, the bond issuer will would need to pay the bond holder a total of $105 when the maturation date of the bond arrives.

The issuer of the bond aims to grow its business or to earn more money from its business activities before the maturation date.

The term of the bond is the time between the date it was issued and the maturity date. There are many things that can happen within the investment term.

For instance, the company could fail and file for bankruptcy. If this is the case, the company and its incorporators are not obliged to pay the creditors (bondholders). This means that you could end up losing your entire investment on the bonds of the said company. This is probably the worst case scenario for the bond holder.

Because of this risk, bonds are categorized, depending on the types of issuer and the level of risk that that the issuer may fail.

Types of Bonds

- *Corporate Bonds vs. Government-Issued Bonds* - These two types of bonds are self-explanatory. Corporate bonds are issued by private companies, while government-issued bonds are issued by the government and government-owned corporations. Generally, corporate bonds are riskier than government-issued bonds because they have a chance of failing and going bankrupt. The government, on the other hand, could just collect more taxes or reallocate its budget to pay off the commitment.

    To encourage investors to buy corporate bonds, companies that issue them usually increase the interest rate offered by their bonds. The higher interest rates mean bigger profits for the investor.

- *Low Risk Bonds* - In the hierarchy of bonds based on the risks involved, government-issued bonds tend to be the least risky. These types of bonds are not as risky because the government always has the means to pay off their creditors using people's taxes.

    Next to government bonds, bonds issued by stable companies are also considered low risk bonds. They are low risk because giant companies are time-tested. They are considered to have superior business processes compared to their smaller counterparts, and are unlikely to become bankrupt. Even if these companies fail to reach their growth targets, they still have the assets to pay off their creditors.

These two types of low risk bonds also come with lower interest rates. Because of their low risk nature, issuers of these bonds are confident that they will still sell their bonds to investors even though they offer low interest rates.

The interests rates of these types of bonds are usually the lowest but the investor will have the peace of mind that the bond issuer will not go belly up before the bond matures.

- *High Risk Bonds* - In contrast, some types of bonds are considered high-risk bonds. Most of these bonds fall under the 'Junk Bond' category. These types of bonds are usually issued by newer companies that are just starting to grow. These companies need additional capitalization to expand their business. However, most investors consider them high risk. Because they are fairly new, their business processes are not yet time-tested. The worth of the company may also be significantly lower compared to blue chip companies.

To encourage investors to buy their bonds so that they can raise the capital needed for growth, these bond issuers usually assign higher interest rates and shorter terms to their bonds.

Managed Investment Funds

Some people also want to participate in securities investments, but they do not necessarily want to spend a lot of time learning and keeping track of the market. If you are one of these people, there are managed investment funds for you.

Managed investment funds facilitate the entire investing process for you. All you need to do is to apply, comply with the requirements, provide the fund, and let the fund manager do his work. In an ideal situation, the fund will grow in value over time. This usually happens to all funds. However, growth in the initial amount of your fund may not be enough.

You want to make sure that the performance of your fund exceed metrics such as the inflation rate for the year, the performance of other similar funds, and the performance of automatic funds like index funds. If any of these metrics outperforms your managed investment fund, then the fund is losing.

You should be critical about the performance of managed investment funds because you are actually paying a regular service fee for keeping your money in the fund.

Mutual Funds

Mutual funds are probably the most popular kind of managed fund because they are designed so that regular working people will be able to participate in the market. You can take part in a mutual fund company by buying fund shares. The price of each share is posted in the mutual fund website every day.

The price fluctuates according to the investing performance of the fund manager. If the fund manager's investing activities do well, the price increases. In contrast, when the activities of the manager lose money for the fund or if the general market performs poorly like in times of recessions, the price of the fund will also go down.

Each mutual fund has an underlying asset or a type of security that it can invest in. An equity mutual fund refers to mutual funds that invest solely in the stock market. A bond fund, on the other hand, invests solely in the bond market. Some funds are categorized as balanced funds.

These types of funds can invest in both the stock market and in bond funds. However, the board of directors of the fund sets the rules on how these funds should be invested so that the fund manager will not be able to expose the investors' money to too much risk.

If you want to take part in a mutual fund, you should research about the historical performance, the performance of the fund manager and the fees of the fund.

After deciding which mutual fund company is right for you, you will need to contact that company to ask for the process of applying as an investor. You will also need to decide on the amount that you want to invest.

Best Practices When Investing in Mutual Funds

1. *Choose the Type of Fund That Best Fits Your Financial Goal* - When you apply to invest on a mutual fund, the representative of the fund will usually work with you to set your financial goal and develop an investing plan. He will guide you in choosing the right type of fund for your goal.

    In particular, they will be interested in the duration based on your goal's deadline. For short term goals, the mutual fund advisers usually recommend low risk funds. They do this because they do not want you to lose money in the short time that your fund is with them. On the other hand, they will allow riskier types of funds for your long term goal. In these types of mutual funds, your capital will have time to recuperate if the market goes down.

2. *Be mindful of the Fees That Come with the Fund* - All types of managed funds have fees. However, the amount varies, depending on the company. The fees charged by mutual fund companies are referred to as loads. There are two type of loads - frontend and backend loads. When buying mutual fund shares, you will need to choose which type of fee you want to implement in your investment.

For frontend load, you pay the fees when you buy the mutual fund shares. The frontend load will be deducted from your initial payment. In most cases, the frontend load is a fixed rate of your buy-in amount. It is rare for a mutual fund company to actually change the load rates.

If you choose to use the frontend load for your investment, you will need to consider the rate when you buy your mutual fund shares. After paying the fee, you will no longer need to pay when withdrawing your money from the fund.

Backend load, on the other hand, is a fee that will be deducted from your fund when you liquidate shares you bought. After selling the mutual fund shares, the company will deduct this fee from the fund before creating a check for it. Backend fees are usually set up so that they decrease over time. The mutual fund companies do this to encourage investors to keep their money in the fund for longer periods of time.

If you choose this type of load/fee, you will not pay anything when you buy mutual fund shares. The rate of the backend load starts high. It could start at 5%, for example. After a certain period, the rate decreases to reward you for your loyalty.

For instance, it could go down to 4% after your first year anniversary in the fund. After the second year, it will go down to 3%. It will continue to go down year after year.

If you keep your funds long enough in the fund, there will come a time when you no longer need to pay fees.

3. *Stay Away from Funds Sold by Solicitors or Sales People* – Ideally, you want to stay away from funds that hire active solicitors to promote their products. You do not want to deal with these companies because the people they hire take a chunk out of your fund or initial payment as their commission or finder's fee.

Funds that do not need to pay solicitors generally perform better because the cost of maintaining the fund is kept low.

4. Enter Any Investment Fund with a Goal and a Timeline in Mind - You should already have a plan when you start your investment. Most people do not make plans when they start their investment.

   They just do it because that is what someone told them to do. If you want to be a successful investor, you should always enter the investment with a goal and a timeline in mind.

   Your real world goal should be converted into a monetary target amount. Your aim when investing is to reach that goal. Most goals also have an end date. Based on this end date, you can determine the general timeline of your goal.

   The shorter your goal timeline, the harder it is for you to reach it in time. It is also more difficult to reach the goal amount if it is too high.

5. *Keep Yourself Aware of the Three Important Factors in Passive Investing* - If you choose the mutual fund route to investing, you are choosing to invest your money passively. This means that you will not actively keep track of what's going on in the market. The fees of mutual funds also prevent you from moving your funds around. Instead, you are planning to put your money in an investment system and

you will wait it out until your goal deadline arrives or until the growth of the fund has allowed you to reach your target, whichever comes first.

In this type of investment, you need to keep track of three important factors that will contribute to the growth of your fund - the amount of capital investment, the rate of return of the fund, and time you have before reaching your goals.

When you are investing actively, you need to keep track of minute details of the investment vehicle. If you are invested in stocks for example, it will serve you well to put a lot of time in researching about the companies you invest in. When investing passively, on the other hand, you only need to keep track of these three factors.

For the first one, the larger the capital amount for the investment, the larger the sum of money you will get when your investment grows. This also means that you are risking a larger amount by exposing it to the market.

Second, you want to invest in an investment vehicle with the highest potential rate of return. You can learn about the potential rate of return of an asset by reviewing its past performance. While economists will argue that past performance is not indicative of future returns, checking the historical records does give you an evidence of what possibly can happen.

It is also important to remember that the rate of return of your fund also depends on the economic cycle that affects its underlying assets. For example, if the mutual fund is invested solely in stocks, you will notice that the historical performance of the fund tends to increase steadily over time.

At every 8-10 year period, you may also notice that there may be a huge dip in the mutual fund performance. This may coincide with major economic downturns like recession or a market crash.

You need to consider the current point in the cycle when you are investing. If you start investing right after a stock market crash or at the start of the recession, you may get the mutual fund shares at a low price. On the other hand, if you start buying in an economic boom, the price of the shares may be too high.

Investing in Securities: Define Your Circle of Influence

Successful investor Warren Buffet made the concept of circle of influence popular. He suggested that each investor should have one.

Buffet explains that the circle of influence refers to a sector in the securities market that you have expert-level knowledge on. As you become more experienced in investing, you become even more knowledgeable of the events going on in these sectors.

When deciding on your circle of influence, it is best to start with the sectors that you are already interested in and that you want to learn more about. You will also spend less time in the learning curve if you choose a sector that you are already knowledgeable about.

When practicing to invest, you could try researching and practice investing in sectors where you work. A doctor for example, would have superior knowledge over the rest of the market when comes to companies that deal with medical supplies. Using his connections in the medical field, the doctor may be able to find information about key companies before the market does.

On the other hand, a person working in a tech-related company, may have superior information gathering skills when it comes to tech companies. The tech sector right now is one of the riskiest to invest in the New York Stock Exchange. If an investor does not know how these technology companies work, it's easy to lose money investing in them.

You become an expert in your circles of influence if you gain and process information faster than the rest of the market.

Let's say that you decided to learn about car manufacturing companies that are listed in the stock exchange. While car companies are as old as the stock exchanges themselves, they evolve over time.

In the past, American and European companies dominated the market. Eventually, they were toppled by the efficient business processes of Japanese car makers. Now, new players are coming in from both Europe and from Asia.

If you want to become an expert in this micro-sector, you will need to keep track of all the car makers in the market. This includes their history, their recent top products, and their market share.

To break it down, you will have to learn about each company's market performance and the things that are happening in each company.

You will also need to take note of the recent movements of the price of the shares of the company and the reasons why these price changes happened. It would also help if you start learning how to read the financial reports and charts of these companies.

For consumer product producing companies like these, a lot of weight is given on the company's share of the market. The top company usually takes more than 50% of the market, with the smaller companies competing for what's left.

Each company in a sector wants to take more of the market share each quarter. You will need to rank these companies according to their dominance in taking the majority of the sales in the market. You should then identify which ones are in a good position to increase their market shares.

You can identify which companies are on their way up the ladder if you study the changes that are happening in each one. The leadership of the company is one of the areas that investors find most interesting. If the board of directors decide to change the CEO for example, the reputation of the new CEO usually affects the prices of the company shares.

If the new CEO has a track record of stabilizing a company and helping them achieve growth goals, the market may respond positively. On the other hand, if the new CEO is untested or has a reputation of taking high risks, the market may have mixed reactions to it and this may reflect in the prices of securities of that company.

Aside from the leadership, you should also learn about the significant changes that are happening within the company's income generating processes. For instance, you should check out the new products that the company has in line.

Companies do not usually release products at the same time to avoid competition. Their new products, however, will always be compared with the latest products of the toughest competitor.

In the smartphone industry for instance, Apple and Samsung are the two biggest players in the market. Whenever Apple releases a new phone, there is no doubt that Samsung's answer will be released soon after.

Whenever Samsung releases its newest product, it is taking a risk. If their products do not work as well as Apple's newest phone, the public may not buy them.

On the other hand, if their phones successfully manage to compete in terms of specs and performance, this may lead to higher sales numbers. This in turn will lead to a higher market share and higher revenue.

When the revenue reports are released, the investors will see that these companies have improved their performance and more of them may buy Samsung stocks. The increased demand in the company stocks will increase share prices.

Investing in Real Estate

Investing in real estate can be another investing option with multiple ways of increasing value to your portfolio. Let's first discuss the different types of real estate properties that you can invest in, depending on the amount of capital you have:

- *Apartment Units and Small Homes* - While there are many other smaller types of investments like renting out lot space for trailer homes, buying apartment units and small homes is probably the best way to start. Most families do not really want to live in trailer parks if they had a choice.

    The majority of your target market wishes to live in a stable apartment or small house. With this type of property, you will have the option to rent them out to individuals, couples, and small families. Such tenants tend to transfer residences a lot in a matter of a few years, giving you the chance to adjust your rent on a regular basis.

- *Suburban Homes* - Next to small homes and apartments, families tend to move to suburban homes near good schools and a commute away from their place of work. Families love these types of homes because they are ideal for raising a child. They usually feature a front and a backyard, as well as enough bedrooms for a regular-size family.

From an investor's perspective, suburban homes are less likely to be rented out unless the spot has a potential to significantly increase in value in the next five years. In most cases, however, suburban homes are best flipped and sold. The investment strategy for this type of property though, will depend on its location.

- *High-End Residential Properties* - The most expensive properties in an area tend to be located in the urban centers. People living in the city do not want to travel all the way from the suburbs to get to work. Instead, they want a living space closer to their places of interest. Condominium units and apartments near population centers in big cities are usually in high demand among those who have money.

In this case, you will need to develop the apartments and other residential properties you find to fit the tastes of your higher end clients. Most clients who can afford the pricy properties in cities like New York or London can keep up with the high price tags as long as the property suits their taste and preferences.

Properties in this market are rarely rented out. If they are, the timeframe for the rent are usually extremely short. Even the ones who just want to live for one to three years in the city will usually buy the place.

If you wish to enter this type of market, you will need the services of real estate brokers who specialize in catering to rich clients. Without a broker of this caliber, you will have difficulty entering the market.

- *Business Properties* - The business property market is even more difficult to penetrate for someone who is just starting out. Businesses are extremely picky in the properties they take. The biggest companies want highly sought after locations like storefronts along busy sidewalks, populated street corners, areas around schools and other busy population centers.

  They are also very critical with the features that come with the building. Some types of business for example, will ask for a specific height from floor to ceiling and specific wall materials.

  If you wish to enter this type of market, you need to be ready to give in to these demands, especially if you have a target client in mind. The locations you get should also fit the needs of the companies you wish to attract.

Now that you know the different types of properties, think of the ones you wish to take part in. When your capital is still low, it is best to stick to the lower priced properties for residential use. As you recover your income, you should aim to grow the number of assets in your portfolio.

How to Earn Using Real Estate

Real properties can increase the value of your investment portfolio in a number of ways. While they will eat a considerable chunk of your capital, investing in properties give you a tangible product that you can work with and improve over time.

- *Capital Appreciation* - Just like all other types of assets, the value of real estate changes over time. Property prices are controlled by supply and demand. People want to buy properties that provide the best benefits based on their lifestyle and personal goals. Businesses, for example, look for locations that will put them in the best position to succeed. Families and individuals, on the other hand, are looking for living spaces that will suit their needs and their budget.

If many buyers want to buy the same property, they compete for it by offering the seller a competitive price. The most determined buyer is expected to give the highest offer. In most cases, this is the offer accepted by the buyer.

The demand in a location tends to be driven by the development in the area. As raw land is developed into an urban landscape, the price of properties in the area also increases. You can choose to sell your property to take advantage of the capital appreciation in the area.

- *Rentals* - Renting a property is the second way of making money from real estate. Rentals usually apply to short term occupancy of a residential or a business area. In population centers like tourist attractions and financial districts, you will often see hotels and other lodging services offered to short term occupants.

    Rentals also apply for monthly payments of residential spaces like houses and apartments. In this way of earning from your property, your tenant signs a contract for the use of the space and the specific landlord-tenant agreement. In some cases, these agreements could also be verbally agreed upon.

    Once the agreement for the rental is set, the occupant uses the space and pays for the rent regularly. While this is the ideal scenario, things do not always go this way. It is common for landlords to meet problematic tenants. This is all part of the business. However, the landlord can prevent this by checking the criminal record and credit history of a prospective occupant.

- *Leases* - Leases are extremely similar to rentals, but they are usually reserved for extremely long term agreements. With a lease, the property owner designs a lease agreement wherein the terms of the lease are provided and the payment amount indicated.

  The duration of leases is usually long term. They could last from a couple of years to even decades. The terms of the lease should also indicate the parts of the property included in the lease and the limitations of the rights of the client. Some leases allow the client to use the entire property with no limitation. The client could build a building in the piece of land he is leasing.

  Other types of leases specify the parts of the property that the client is allowed to use. A client, for instance, may be allowed to use the entire second floor of a building. Some special types of leases have extremely limited scope. A marketing company could lease a hole in the ground so that they will be allowed to stick a street sign. They could also lease the entire side of a building to attach a billboard to it.

Step 3

Collecting Information

Investing is all about acting on the right information in the market. Before you invest, you need to hone your information gathering skills. Your goal is to find actionable information that you can use to answer to the following questions:

Which asset will give the best rate of return?

Which asset has the lowest risk?

When should you start and stop investing in these assets?

After picking the asset that you wish to invest in, you must learn how you can start investing in it. You also want to learn when the best time to start will be. There are a few factors that you can use to arrive at the answers to these questions:

Researching for the Right Time to Buy

Timing is essential in all types of investment. The simplest way to invest is to buy assets when they are priced low and to sell them at a higher price. There are times when most of the assets on the market are just too overpriced. This happens when the market is booming.

This is common in the real estate market. You will notice, for instance, that a plot of land that may have mostly been ignored 5 to 10 years ago is now in demand in the market. The price of this piece of land may skyrocket to up to 500% of its initial price.

This happens when the government or big real estate development corporations start to invest in the said location. If you observe this happening in your area, this may mean that you are already too late in the real estate market. The area may already be attracting too many buyers. More buyers usually mean higher prices if you apply the laws of supply and demand.

When gathering information, you want to go to the sources that provide you with rumored plans of major players in the market. In the scenario above, for example, it would help if you know people in the government or the major real estate development corporations who could share development plans with you.

Having sources who can provide you with actionable information regarding the assets that you are interested in will help you time your entry in the market.

The use of connections as sources of information can be a gray area in investing because it can be prohibited in some types of investments, especially when investing in securities.

The securities and exchange commissions in all countries are always on the lookout for insider trading. This is the act of using confidential information to gain the upper hand in the stock market. In this case, using resource people can lead to some jail time.

Researching the True Value of Assets

You can still time your entry to the stock market without using insider trading. One of the best ways is by investing in companies that are undervalued. Undervalued companies are those whose stock prices are lower than the intrinsic value of the company.

In the stock market, the price of stocks is determined by the market. If there are more buyers than sellers in the market, the price tends to go up. While in theory, the average price of a stock is indicative of its true price of the shares of the company, this is not always the case. Some economists declare that the price of stocks is always wrong and that the market is always attempting to correct it.

Certain factors though, like the current market situation, unfortunate incidents about the company, the popularity of competing companies and the marketing strategies of the said company can affect the market price of the stock. Your goal as an investor is to find stocks whose prices are below their correct price.

The intrinsic value of the company can be measured based on many factors. One is the actual means of production of the company. A car manufacturing company, for instance, may have a sufficient number of factories to produce double the amount they are producing right now.

A simple change in leadership or in the marketing strategy can lead to higher revenue. This gives the company a higher intrinsic value than its price indicates.

Another factor for finding out intrinsic value is its earning potential. The earnings trend of the company is an important indicator of its health. A company whose earnings are rising year after year has the potential to grow even bigger. With growth in the company come higher stock prices.

Factors like a bad economy, accidents within the company or the presence of strong competition in the market, can distract many investors from putting money on these companies. Because of this, the stock price of the company may not rise at all even with strong performance in the revenue report.

You could also check the underlying technology behind the product of a company. If you are a product expert, you may have an eye for high quality products that may do well on the market.

Some companies have developed technologies that can work well in the market. People's lack of familiarity of the said technology may prevent the stock prices of these companies from rising.

Your goal when researching is to look at the new products of companies in the sector you've chosen. You could then compare them with the other technological assets that other companies also have.

If you can find companies with promising technology to back up their product, you may be able to beat other investors by investing in these companies while their prices are still low.

Researching about the Right Time to Exit the Market

You should also plan when you will sell your assets and make profits. Knowing when to liquidate your assets is just as important as knowing when to buy.

Before we proceed with the discussion though, it is important to be aware of one of the ideal mindsets to have when in the process of buying assets. This mindset is closely related to when you are going to liquidate the assets you have obtained in the past.

When investing, keep a goal oriented mindset. Each of your investment funds placed in different assets must have a goal associated with it. Your decision on when to liquidate the asset will always depend on this goal. Most of the important goals in our lives have a financial system for them set up by the government. In the US, we have the 401k and similar investment programs for our retirement.

Banks and other financial institutions set up college funds for the high cost of tertiary education. These types of investment funds though, will not make you rich. They are only there to aid you in reaching your basic goals of meeting your life needs.

In previous chapters, we have discussed that when buying high risk assets, it is important to use only the money that is not intended for important goals. Funds like the ones set aside for your children's college education, your retirement, and your home mortgage should be kept in low risk investment plans.

These goals have a fixed timeline and putting these funds in high risk investments could jeopardize your plans, subsequently ruin your life.

Instead, the money that you put on the stock market and other high risk types of assets must be set for one goal, and that is maximum growth. With this goal, you are free to chase after high risk investment decisions that have the potential for high returns.

You should still do your due diligence and research as much as you can for actionable information about the asset. In short, do not be reckless when investing in high risk assets.

By having a different fund for high risk assets, you will be able to act freely without being bothered by the pressure that comes with your important life goals. The best example of this happened during the pre-recession boom between 2006 and 2007.

The market was already picking up because people started refinancing their properties. A lot of the cash created by the refinancing activities went to consumer spending.

As a result, the stock prices generally increased in the New York Stock Exchange. At the peak of the economic boom, many people thought that they could make quick money by taking part in the stock market. Many of these people though, were too late and did not realize that the market was being fed by a real estate bubble that was about to burst.

The media also did not help by reporting as if the boom was going to last forever.

Some of the latecomers used funds from important goals to participate in the market. When the market crashed in 2008, everybody wanted out. People started selling their assets in an attempt to cut their losses.

Unfortunately, for most people, it was too late, and the damage had already been done. A great chunk of the funds intended for their important goals vanished as the market corrected the overvaluing of the market that was caused by the real estate bubble.

Using the tips in this book will prevent you from falling into this trap. Most of the people who invested prior to the market collapse of 2008 would have been able to prevent big losses by keeping their money in the market for one or two more years. However, many of them acted based on fear and sold their shares. They were afraid that their losses would only get bigger if they stayed even just a little longer.

If you have a separate fund just for your high risk investment, you need to avoid acting based on fear. Instead of pulling your money out when the market goes down, you will be able to change your strategy to minimize your losses.

If you lost 30% of your fund in a market crash, for example, you will not immediately withdraw your money and finalize your losses.

In fact, by doing so, you will incur even more losses in the form of additional transaction and service fees. Instead of liquidating your assets based on fear, you will instead assess the situation and create a new strategy on dealing with the change in the market.

In this scenario, you will only need to withdraw your money if the assets you are holding are fundamentally low in value and does not stand a chance of recovering from the crash. If the company has a solid hold in the market, the effects of the crash will only be temporary. In one or two years, the stock prices of the solid company should be able to recover, or even rise to a level beyond the pre-crash stock prices.

You will heavily rely on your research to come up with this decision. Based on the tips in this book, we only recommend buying high quality assets. However, you may find yourself accidentally holding on to assets with lower quality at a time of a market crash. These types of assets will be hard-pressed to recover in these kinds of scenarios.

You will have to research on a company's ability and chances of recovering from a downturn. This way, you will be able to come up with a profitable decision on whether to sell or hold.

Step 4

Taking Action. Starting Investing

Now, you have all the information you need to start investing. You have assessed your current financial situation. You have chosen the assets to invest in, and you have done sufficient research. It's time to actually start your journey as an investor.

In this chapter, we will discuss the different steps that you need to take to start your investing activities, regardless of the investment vehicle that you chose in the previous chapters:

1. *Collecting Capital* - The first task when investing is knowing where you will get your capital. Most people use their own money to start. This is necessary for some investment activities like investing in securities. Ideally, you should use cash for securities, and there is no better source of cash than your own savings. As mentioned in the previous chapters, you could use your extra cash for this purpose. If you receive a bonus or an unexpected extra income, you

could put that amount in your high risk investment fund.

Loans are perfectly acceptable for some types of investments. This is particularly useful if you choose to invest in real estate properties or if you choose to set up and start your own business. You can also collect money from other investors who may be willing to put money on your proposed ventures. To get capital this way, you will need to approach potential investors and pitch them your plan for investing in real estate, or for putting up your own business.

In major investing cities like New York, London and Toronto, you will find many people who have the cash to fund your business ventures. It's just a matter of convincing them that your investment plan will work, and will be worth investing on.

Even if you are not in these cities though, you can still approach other people to fund your plans. For instance, you can start with interested friends and family members. You can also make use of the power of the internet through crowd sourcing. America is the leading country when it comes to outsourcing startups. Many people are looking for ideas to fund. Just like with individual investors, you just have to create a package to offer the crowd for them to start investing in your ideas.

2. *Connect with the Right Professionals -* After collecting the necessary capital for your investment, the next step is to gather your team. In most types of investments, you will not be able to do it alone. You will either need to work with a professional in the field that you wish to participate in or work with a service that will facilitate for you.

In real estate for example, you usually need to work with a real estate broker. This professional is licensed to promote and facilitate the sale of your property. If you are flipping properties, you may also need to work with people who will help you make repairs and do property feature upgrades, depending on what the property needs to increase its value.

If you are planning to start investing in securities, on the other hand, you will need to work with the right broker or investing service. In the stock market, for instance, you will need to work with stock brokers. These people are licensed to facilitate the buying and selling of company stocks listed in the stock exchange. They can also give you some expert advice on how to invest, and which stocks to buy or sell.

If you are planning to put your money into managed accounts or automated investment funds like the index fund, you will need to connect with the right investment fund company. These companies make the investment process for you. Usually, they are easy to contact and you can visit them in their offices. They usually have an office conveniently located near the areas they are operating in.

These firms are also the leading providers of online services in the industry. They provide you with a way to invest in the assets they offer even if you cannot physically go to their office.

In this case, you may be required to provide documentation as proof of your identity and income. These are required by law to make sure that your sources of income are legitimate and that you are not laundering other people's money.

As mentioned in previous chapters, you want to discuss the fees of these professionals and investment services before you start working with them. Make sure that you understand these fees so that you will be able to accurately predict how much your potential income will be.

3. *Design Your Own Investing Strategy* - Now that you have the right professionals in your

corner, you can now start investing. Regardless of the type of asset that you have selected to put your funds in, you still need to make other important decisions.

When investing in the stock market, for instance, you will need to make the decision of which companies, sector or index to invest in. You also need to plan how long you will hold the asset and how much of your funds you will commit to that asset.

In the real estate market, on the other hand, you will need to decide on whether you want to buy a residential or a business property. You also need to make a plan on how you are going to make money with it. Are you going to rent it out or sell it for a profit?

These decisions are crucial to make sure that you make a profit in all of your investment activities. Without a clear plan from the beginning, you will end up making rushed decisions that may lead to losses.

Remember to stick to your target amount for funds that are committed to specific life goals. Once you reach your target amount, you should force yourself to liquidate the assets and withdraw your money.

You could be greedier with your high-risk investment funds. This fund is designed to make you rich, rather than just to reach specific life goals. You want to maximize the growth of these fund so you can accumulate as much profit as you want and need.

4. *Buy the Right Types of Assets Based on Your Research* - At this stage, you will need to work closely with the professionals that you partnered with so you can maximize your profit. It is also crucial that you get all the assets at the right price.

Many people make the mistake of buying overpriced assets in their first outing. It is difficult to make a profit from these assets. Instead, you want to keep the prices as low as possible. This can lead to bigger profits later.

While it is important is to listen to your advisers, you will also need to do your own research so that you can adjust your strategies according to the prevailing conditions of the market. You will need to keep track of all the factors related to the asset that you bought.

If you are invested in the stock market, for example, you should know as much as you can about the activities going on within that company without breaking the law. You also need to keep track of the financial reports they release to the public.

While reading financial reports is important, they rarely provide you with predictive information that can help you make the right decisions ahead of the market. To know how the market will generally respond to reports that are just about to come out, you will need to be creative on where you get your information.

For instance, if you are invested in the pharmaceutical sector, it helps if you put a lot of effort in learning about the sales performance of the products of the companies you is invested in.

Let's say you bought stocks of Company A, a drug manufacturing company, three months ago. At the time when you bought them, the company was releasing a new stress-relief medication, and the anticipation of the product drove the stock prices higher. Three months after launching the new product, Company A is about to release its next quarterly sales numbers to the investors.

Investors usually look forward to these kinds of reports because the information they contain helps them decide on whether they should hold on to the company's stocks or not. In your case, you can save a lot of money if you find information that will indicate the likely sales numbers of the company.

You should then compare this to the anticipated sales number in the media. The anticipated sales numbers are usually based on the projected growth of the company, which is released to the investors in the beginning of the fiscal year.

If Company A meets or exceeds its target sales numbers, its stock prices may continue to go up. If the sales numbers, on the other hand, are less than the target amount, the market may respond by unloading their stocks. This will lead to a dip in the stock prices.

In your case, you want to make the decision even before the sales report comes out. You can do this by gathering information from other sources in the industry. People in the industry generally have an idea if a new product is a boom or a bust by analyzing how the new product from Company A performed in the last three months in terms of sale.

You can also apply the same strategy in real estate. When investing in real property, you will know if you are too late in the market if the prices of properties have significantly increased over a short period of time. This means that the general market is already in the know of the upward trend of the property prices in the area. People and companies alike are already starting to look for properties to buy in the area to take part in the development boom.

As an investor, you do not necessarily want to look for properties whose prices are already trending upward. Instead, you want to get properties at a low price. You don't have to settle with just any property, though. You want to find properties that have a great potential to increase in value within a short period of time.

To find such properties, you will need to build your connections in the real estate world, in particular, in the area where you want to buy properties. If you want to find a property to buy in New York for example, you can start by connecting with real estate brokers who have properties to sell. These people try to find the best properties in the area and list them in their own inventory. You could tell them your plan and ask if they could show you some of the properties that are available for sale.

Step 5

Expanding Your Investments

In the previous chapter, you took your first baby steps in the world of investing. You researched on the right types of assets based on your goals and preferences. You tried out acquiring select investments, and you now have a few assets in your portfolio - whether they are stocks, bonds, precious metals, commodities or real estate properties.

To achieve your ultimate goal of getting rich faster, your next step will be to expand your portfolio. This means going back and repeating the steps we have discussed in the first few chapters in choosing the investments to add to your existing assets.

Adding More Money to Your Investment Portfolio

Obviously, to start increasing the total value of your investments, you need to put in more money. There are many ways on how you can do this. You can use your extra income to buff up your investment portfolio. If you currently don't have any additional sources of income, you need to actively look for them. Generally, you want to increase your productivity so that you will have more money to use for investing.

Over time, when your investment portfolio starts to earn money for you, it will be able to fund your needs, and the amount of work you have to put in will also decrease. More importantly, you will be able to set aside money for savings or for future investments.

If you are an employee like 90% of the rest of the people reading this book, you may use cost averaging to start increasing your total capital amount. (Refer to the appropriate section in Step 1 to refresh your memory about cost averaging.)

You could do this by setting aside a specific amount from your regular income to be committed to your investment portfolio. Ideally, you should put at least 20% of your income for this purpose.

Let's say you receive $2,000 every month. Instead of spending all the money you earn in one go, you can allot 20% or about $400 to your investment funds. If 20% is too high for now, you can adjust it so that it suits your current financial situation. You can just increase the allocation when your financial condition improves.

Making the Right Decisions

After allotting a specific amount of your income to your investment portfolio, you need to create a strategy on how you will distribute the money to the various types of security you wish to invest in. The best strategy for you will depend on the information you have gathered from the previous steps.

Let's say you started investing in stocks and you have reason to believe that the company whose stocks you own is about to become popular in the market. In this case, you may choose to buy more stocks, and increase the number of shares you own in that company.

On the other hand, if you think that there is a bubble in the market, and it may burst anytime soon, you could lessen your exposure in the stock market to protect your investment. In this case, you may choose to find other investment vehicles to put your money in. The best choice is usually to put your newly collected money in the bank if you are not sure what investment type to start with next.

However, bear in mind that you should only retain the money from your high-risk fund in the bank for short time periods. Leave your money there just until you find a new investment vehicle that you can use as a safe haven.

The usual safe havens are low risk funds like money market funds and high quality bonds (government issued bonds or blue chip company bonds). Gold is also a popular safe haven when high risk markets like the stock exchange begin to slump. The slumping of the stock market usually happens because the biggest investors in the said market tend to transfer their investments to low risk assets. This option is also available for you.

If you chose to initially invest in real estate, it is highly likely that you have already used up much of your liquid assets in buying the real estate property. The additional assets you add to your portfolio should be committed to creating more value and gaining income from the properties you bought.

You can add value to the property by spending some money to develop it. If it is already developed, you can still add value to it by fixing even minor problems and issues with the property, and making it more livable.

Step 6

Diversifying Your Portfolio

In the previous chapter, we discussed how you can steadily increase the value of your investment portfolio. So far though, you have only put your money in one or a few types of asset. Putting your money in one type of asset can work if your portfolio size is still small. However, as the total value of your portfolio increases, putting them all in one asset endangers much of your fund to unforeseen circumstances that may have a significant negative impact.

Let's say you started investing in the stock market. After 6 months of using cost averaging to increase the value of your stock portfolio, you noticed that the portfolio size is already becoming too big. If you do not redistribute your funds, it will only take one major dip in the market to wipe out a big chunk of your investment.

If you invested solely in the stock market in 2007 for instance, you would have lost 30%-50% of the value of your portfolio in 2008. On the other hand, if half of your money was invested in gold, you would have saved 1/3 to ½ of the money you would have lost.

The ideal thing to do when your portfolio size is growing is to reallocate your assets with the goal of diversifying them. Investment analysts usually refer to the saying of 'putting all your eggs in one basket' when teaching diversification of assets. If an egg farmer puts all of his eggs in just one basket, he may lose all of the eggs if the basket rips apart or if something happens to it while it is being transported.

On the other hand, if you put your eggs in separate baskets, and let two different people carry each basket, you will be able to save one of the baskets in case something happens to the other carrier.

The same thing applies when investing. If you keep all your money in one type of asset, you are in danger of losing a large chunk, if not all of it, if something bad happens. Let's say that there is an economic bubble in the stock market that the experts failed to detect and the media failed to report. Most of your funds would still be in the market when the bubble bursts. All of your money invested in the said market will be subject to the decrease in the value of the assets.

To protect your money from events like these, you should diversify and have a proper distribution of your funds. First, let's discuss the different types of distribution of funds:

- *In-Market Diversification* - Even if you choose to invest all your money in just one asset market, you can still practice diversification. Instead of buying stocks from just one company, you can distribute your investment funds to many companies in the stock exchange. Instead of putting all your money in one sector or industry, you can distribute it among many industries that you are familiar with. If one company falls, the rest of your funds will still be protected because you distributed it to many companies in the market.

- *Inter-Market Diversification* - Inter-market diversification refers to the practice of putting your money in different types of assets. For instance, you can distribute your funds among bonds, stocks, real estate and precious metals. In the beginning, you can start with one type of asset while your portfolio size is still small. At this stage, you can execute an in-market diversification to protect your money from small disasters within the market. As it grows in value, you can choose to liquidate some of it and transfer it to a second type of asset. You will need to study the second type of asset before you start buying it. This will ensure that you know what you are doing coming in. You also need to develop your entry and exit plan, just like you did with your first asset.

If you started investing in the stock market, you could transition to buying real estate to diversify your portfolio. You can choose to liquidate your assets and start buying real property. You may then use this second asset to earn more passive income through rentals, leases, and other forms of income generating activities.

- *Inter-Country Diversification* - When you become a successful investor, there may come a time when your portfolio may grow too big. This usually happens when a country experiences an economic boom. The skillful investors of that country begin to accumulate wealth distributed in many types of assets.

   Even with proper intermarket diversification, your money is still exposed to risks. Most of the investment markets within a country are interconnected. If one of them crashes, the others are usually affected as well. In 2007, for instance, the crash first started in the real estate market. Because they are interconnected, the stock market was also greatly affected, leading to price dips all across the board, even to companies that are remotely connected to real estate.

To further protect your money from unforeseen events, you can also invest in funds that are invested in other countries. If you have family relations in other countries, you can start learning about the investment markets they have there.

You can also look into the different ways on how you can invest in the securities and other types of assets in these countries. A lot of companies welcome foreign investors.

For you, it's just a matter of going through the right channels and decreasing the total fees you need to pay.

The easiest way for you to take part in the growth of other countries is by finding an investment fund whose underlying assets are focused in these countries. Some mutual funds, for instance, invest in specific regions like the Euro, East Asian, and South East Asian regions. You can also take part in commodities trading of supplies that originate from other countries.

Step 7

Aiming for Durable Passive Income Generating Assets

If you have been reading investment related content for a while, you may already be familiar with investors' obsession with passive income. To become rich, you also want to gain assets that produce this type of income. Let's talk about what it is and how you can gain assets that generate it.

Passive Income

Passive income is, simply put, income that you do not work for to obtain. In a regular 9-5 job, you are paid hourly. When employed, the amount of income you get is proportionate to the number of hours you've worked in a given period. You may also increase it with better productivity.

With passive income, most of the work comes at the beginning, and you are not immediately paid for it. When you start a business for instance, you are required to spend money, do research, and set up the different aspects of your business to start earning money. The same goes with investing. You first need to do research on the companies that you want to invest in, start building your connections in the industry, accumulate capital, and buy assets. The major difference though, is that the work significantly lessens over time when investing.

1. *Passive Income through Stocks* - After doing research and buying the right stocks for example, you may get dividends from the stocks you own. You can use these dividends to buy more stocks or you can cash them out, and use the proceeds for your needs.

    Setting up passive income streams is best done when you are planning to retire. In the beginning of your investment career, you should first focus on growth. You may still be working at this point and you can use your salary as your source of income. You can use the strategies discussed in the previous chapters to make your investments grow.

    After the growth stage of your investment journey, and you already want to retire, you can liquidate your faster growing assets that do not give out dividends and buy stocks that do. You can also buy preferred stocks. As discussed in a previous chapter, preferred shares of stock may pay regular dividends. This way, you will receive regular payments from the stocks you own.

2. *Earning Passive Income from Properties* - Aside from stocks, you should also consider buying asset types that could be turned into businesses. Real estate properties for instance may be rented out to set up a regular passive income stream.

You can choose between residential or business properties, depending on the area where you wish to operate. Aside from the living and business spaces, there are other aspects of the property that you can monetize. If the property you own is along a busy highway, you can also add a billboard on its side for added income.

You can also monopolize the services and supply of resources in your properties. If you own an apartment building for example, consider adding a grocery store at first floor. You can make the tenants pay for laundry as well as for cleaning services.

You may think that all these income ideas will require you to work. The secret to getting passive income is to hire someone competent. You will basically need a property manager who will look after your assets. If you have too many properties, you may need to hire more than one.

The property manager will do various tasks for you like collect the rent, take care of repairs, handle complaints, and deal with other concerns of the tenants. With a competent property manager by your side, you will be able to free your time and enjoy your retirement while collecting passive income. You will need to check your properties regularly, and make sure that your assets are in good shape.

3. *Funding Businesses* - If you are into supporting small businesses, you can also help startups get off the ground by funding them. Many people have excellent ideas for a business. Their biggest problem usually revolves around getting enough funding. You can take the role of an investor to these starting businesses.

    Aside from money, these people will need your guidance and your connections to make their business work. After helping them get their business off the ground, you are free to take your portion of the profits.

    Make sure that the agreement between you and the business owners are clear by stating what you will be offering and what rate of return you will be expecting from them. All these should be written in a contract or agreement.

    Funding businesses is extremely risky because many of them require a long time before they can recoup the capital investment. If the capital runs out before they get a solid foothold in the market they are serving, the business is in danger of going bankrupt, and you will have no way of getting your money back. To ensure that this does not happen to you, make sure to practice due diligence when looking for a startup to fund.

TV shows like Shark Tank have made the venture capitalist popular. However, TV shows fail to display the level of scrutiny that real venture capitalists practice when studying a business. They do not just say yes right after they hear a pitch. In reality, venture capitalists first study the business process of a prospect before they actually say yes. They do this by learning as much as they can about the product, its limitations, and its value in the market.

Because of the limitations of your own fund, you will need to turn down the majority of the business pitches you will get. To find the best opportunity for investing, you should start by looking at the unique products of the businesses around your home town. Simple homemade products could now be sold nationally using fulfillment systems offered by companies like Amazon. With the internet, a small manufacturing company can reach millions of consumers that they would not have reached otherwise.

4. *Real Estate Investment Trusts (REITs)* - Being part of an REIT is also a good way to earn an income passively. REITs are companies that collect funds from investors and invest them in a group of real properties. These companies mostly buy urban properties that could be used both for residential and business purposes. The value of the share of the company increases with the success of the properties bought by the trust.

   It is important to remember that the number of properties of an REIT is not necessarily indicative of its ability to make money. It all boils down to the income of each property owned by the trust, and the efficiency of how these properties are managed.

   Just like with all other asset types listed in this book, you will need to do your due diligence as an investor, and try to find all the information that you can about the REIT you want to join. Some of these REITs are listed in the stock exchange and you may be able to gain information about them through the financial records they release regularly.

5. *Limited Partnerships* - You can also take part in limited partnerships or LP. An LP is a type of business wherein many investors pool their money together to acquire assets that they would not be able to afford if they

were alone. The number of investors varies. However, each of them will get shares of the assets acquired by the partnership. The percentage of ownership is usually adjusted according to the amount contributed by the partner.

This type of partnership could apply to buying a group of small businesses, real properties and other types of income generating assets. Each partner in this case gets a portion of the income of the asset and its liquidated value. In this type of business agreement, one of the partners usually takes charge in the management of the asset. The managing partner is paid a salary and also gets his share from the partnership.

Just like with investing in startups, the success of a limited partnership greatly depends on the underlying asset well as in the management of the asset. If the underlying asset is not very profitable, the partners may not be able to get their investment back. At the same time, they will not get the expected passive income from the asset.

The management of the asset could also affect its earning. If the managing partner makes the wrong decisions in developing the asset, the capital raised by the partnership may be used up with no asset to show for it. It is important that the partners choose a manager who has the experience and the skills to create a profitable asset.

To start your own limited partnership, you can begin by looking for an asset that you wish to start with. You can then look for like-minded people or capitalists who wish to be part of the partnership. Lastly, you will need to find a manager who is skilled enough to manage the spending of the capital and maintain the asset.

6. *Bonds and Debentures* - Bonds and related assets have been discussed in detail in past chapters. In this section, we will only discuss their potential as a source of passive income. You do not have to buy bonds when they are released. You can also buy them from the bonds market.

The passive income from bonds comes in the form of the investment payment. The issuers of bonds need to pay the bondholder the annual interest rate. This payment is done semiannually and it could be a good source of passive income.

As discussed in previous chapters, the danger with investing in bonds comes with the quality of the issuer. If you are looking into investing only in high quality bonds, you may be surprised at how low their interest rates are. If you wish to get higher interest rates from the bond market, you will need to consider medium and high risk bond issuers.

7. *Peer to Peer Lending* - P2P or peer to peer lending is a relatively new asset to invest in. In this system of lending, firms facilitate the lending between you as the creditor and whoever the borrower will be. You can invest as low as $25 and it will be returned to you with the advertised interest. The borrower will need to pay a portion of it monthly until their debt is paid. On your end, you slowly get your money back with the corresponding interest.

While peer to peer lending is becoming more popular by the day, it is by no means a foolproof means of investing. The firms that manage these peer to peer lending systems have a short track record for investors to rely on.

The popularity of P2P is currently limited in the US. A few of the US firms have transitioned into Canada. Their profitability though remains to be determined.

Conclusion

I hope this book was able to help you to learn how you can become rich by investing your money wisely.

To recap, here are the 7 steps that we have thoroughly discussed in the book:

Step 1: Assessing Your Financial Situation - You first need to come up with a realistic assessment of your current financial condition. This way you will know how much you can afford to invest. It doesn't matter if you think you do not have enough money to start investing. You can always build a foundation by starting small.

Step 2: Picking Your Assets – Here you will look for suitable assets considering the amount you have put aside for your first investments. Even if you do not have much in the beginning, it is important to start so that you can build up as soon as possible.

Step 3: Collecting Information - Before putting money on your chosen asset, you must dedicate some time to learn everything you can about that particular asset. This will help you to take informed decisions when buying those assets.

Step 4: Taking Action. Starting Investing - By now, you are already prepared to make your first investments. You have set aside an investing fund and have done all due research about the asset you have chosen. It is time now to buy and invest.

Step 5: Expanding Your Investments - You have previously made your first investments. Based on your assessment on the performance of your initial investment, you can buy more of it or consider buying other similar assets.

Step 6: Diversifying Your Portfolio - You are now aware that each investment comes with inherent risks. Thus, you need to diversify your portfolio in order to protect your total capital. By doing this, you will be covered whenever one asset depreciates compared to another.

Step 7: Aiming for Durable Passive Income Generating Assets - While you may have solid assets in your portfolio like gold and retirement plans, your ultimate goal of building riches will only be achieved when your assets can produce a steady stream of passive income.

Unless you inherit a fortune or win the lottery, you cannot expect to get rich overnight. Getting rich takes time, discipline, and effort. By following the 7 steps provided in this book, you will slowly build your wealth, and get rich before you reach your retirement age.

The earlier you begin investing, the bigger your potential returns will be. If you experience some sort of learning curve in the beginning, don't worry. This is normal. The important thing is that you learn from your experiences, and you continue working towards you goal.

To your success!

Other Books by Erick Walk

Available on CreateSpace and Kindle

www.ingramcontent.com/pod-product-compliance
Lightning Source LLC
Chambersburg PA
CBHW050114230526
45470CB00004B/1835